Dieser Katalog erscheint anläßlich der Ausstellungen
im April/Mai 1986:

KUNSTRAUM MÜNCHEN

KUNSTFORUM
Städtische Galerie im Lenbachhaus

Für Unterstützung danken wir der
Galerie Emmerich – Baumann, Zürich

Herausgeber:

KUNSTRAUM MÜNCHEN
Vorstand: Dr. Michael Tacke (Vorsitz), Dr. Luise Horn,
Erik Mosel, Christine Tacke

Katalog:
Christine Tacke (Konzeption und Redaktion)

Fotos:
D. James Dee, New York (Abb./Fig. 10, 17, 22)
Gaechter + Clahsen, Zürich (Abb. 24, 30, 31)
Yoram Lehmann, Jerusalem (alle übrigen)
Meidad Suchowolski, New York (Abb. 1, 2, 3, 18, 19, 20)

Übersetzungen:
John Ormrod (aus dem Deutschen)
Christine Tacke (aus dem Englischen)

Herstellung:
Jakob Miller und Christine Tacke

Lithos:
Repro Center, München

Druck:
Spengler & Stulz GmbH

Auflage: 1200 Exemplare

ISBN: 3-923874-54-5

Michael Gitlin

KUNSTRAUM MÜNCHEN

KUNSTFORUM
Städtische Galerie im Lenbachhaus

INHALT / CONTENTS

1   Broken Infinity 1986, Modell

CHRISTINE TACKE

Michael Gitlin in München

Michael Gitlin zeigt im April 1986 neueste Arbeiten in München. Geplant war die Installation *Nostalgia* im Kunstforum, eine Zeichnungsausstellung im Lenbachhaus und die Installation *Broken Infinity* im KUNSTRAUM MÜNCHEN. Aus organisatorischen Gründen mußte die Ausstellung im Lenbachhaus abgesagt werden. Um Michael Gitlin dennoch ausreichend vorstellen zu können, wurden die Pläne geändert. Im KUNSTRAUM MÜNCHEN sind nun Zeichnungen und Skulpturen zu sehen.

Das Modell von *Broken Infinity* (Abb. 1) soll hier aber vorgestellt werden, da die Arbeit so exakt für den KUNSTRAUM MÜNCHEN konzipiert worden ist, daß sie wahrscheinlich an keinem anderen Ort mehr realisiert werden wird.

Es sollte eine Unendlichkeitsschleife durch alle Räume gebaut werden, nicht aus einem Stück, sondern aus dicken Balken (20 x 20 cm) sichtbar zusammengesetzt. Statt der eleganten mathematischen Formel der Unendlichkeit sollte ein sperriges Gebilde zu sehen sein, das sich dem Auge widersetzt. Die Schleife sollte nicht in einer Ebene verlaufen, sondern – gestützt von einfachen Holzscheren – raumgreifend auf- und absteigen, dabei auch eine Wand durchstoßen. Die kräftige grüne Farbe auf dem Holz sollte einen harten Kontrast zum Weiß der Räume abgeben. Von keiner Stelle in den Räumen sollte das Ganze als Unendlichkeitsschleife kenntlich sein, nur Fragmente einer rätselhaften Konstruktion hätte der Betrachter gesehen. Nur mit größter Anstrengung wäre daraus die Unendlichkeitsschleife erkennbar gewesen.

Bei diesem Erkennungsprozeß der Form wird gleichzeitig die philosophische und die naturwissenschaftliche Frage nach der Unendlichkeit gestellt, vom Sichtbaren auf das Unsichtbare geschlossen, von der Erscheinung auf die Idee. Neben der Endlichkeit jedes einzelnen Menschen auf dieser Welt steht die Frage, ob es eine Unendlichkeit des Kosmos gibt. Ist unsere Endlichkeit ein Fragment der Unendlichkeit?

Blaise Pascal sagt dazu:
„Bedenke ich die kurze Dauer meines Lebens, aufgezehrt von der Ewigkeit vorher und nachher; bedenke ich das bißchen Raum, den ich einnehme, und selbst den, den ich sehe, verschlungen von der unendlichen Weite der Räume, von denen ich nichts weiß und die von mir nichts wissen, dann erschaudere ich und staune, daß ich hier und nicht dort bin; keinen Grund gibt es, weshalb ich gerade hier und nicht dort bin, weshalb jetzt und nicht dann. Wer hat mich hier eingesetzt? Durch wessen Anordnung und Verfügung ist mir dieser Ort und diese Stunde bestimmt worden? *Memoria hospitis unius diei praetereuntis.* (Und wie man einen vergißt, der nur einen Tag Gast gewesen ist, Weisheit Salomons, 5.15)"[1]

Die Erkenntnisse der Naturwissenschaften über den Kosmos[2] haben bis jetzt jedenfalls dazu geführt, daß unser Weltbild immer wieder erschüttert, verunsichert wird, daß es zerfällt und neu gedacht werden muß.[3]

Immer deutlicher wird, daß unser fragmenthaftes Wissen von den Dingen die Sehnsucht nach einer den Kosmos umfassenden Harmonie wachsen läßt. Es ist die Vision von einer Vollkommenheit, in der sich alle Teile zu einem Ganzen fügen.

Die meisten Skulpturen von Michael Gitlin bestehen aus Fragmenten, die sich gedanklich ergänzen lassen, ja die Ergänzung herausfordern. Die Installation *Broken Infinity* dagegen hätte ein fragmentiertes Ganzes gezeigt – ein neuer Aspekt seiner Arbeit.

Die Zeichnungen von Michael Gitlin geben ein wenig von den fragmentierten Linien wieder. Oft versuchen die Linien, die immer wieder unterbrochen und neu angesetzt werden, sich durchzusetzen in einer bestimmten Ebene. Andere Linien fahren dazwischen, ein Streit um die Ebenen setzt ein, man hat das Gefühl, die Linien wollen aus ihrer planen Dimension in die zweite Dimension des Raumes ausbrechen. Nahes rückt in den Hintergrund, von dort wollen Linien sich in den Vordergrund schieben. Ihre ständige Unruhe zieht den Betrachter in ihren Raum.

[1] Blaise Pascal, Gedanken, übersetzt von Ewald Wasmuth, Ziffer 205, nach L. Brunschwicg, Stuttgart 1956; Originaltext s. S. 10, Fußnote 1

[2] Zu den neuesten Erkenntnissen der Kosmologie s. Edward R. Harrison, Kosmologie, 2. Auflage, Darmstadt 1984

[3] Die Annahme eines Urknalls erklärt noch nicht, was davor war (Entstehung aus dem Nichts, aus dem Vakuum?), noch, ob der Kosmos sich immer weiter ausdehnt oder wieder in sich zusammenfällt, zu Nichts wird.

CHRISTINE TACKE
Michael Gitlin in Munich

Michael Gitlin's Munich exhibition in April 1986 is devoted to the artist's most recent work. The original intention was to show the installation *Nostalgia* in the Kunstforum, a collection of drawings in the Lenbachhaus, and the installation *Broken Infinity* in the KUNSTRAUM MÜNCHEN. However, organizational difficulties led to the cancellation of the Lenbachhaus exhibition, which meant that the plans had to be changed in order to ensure an adequate presentation of Gitlin's work. The exhibition in the KUNSTRAUM MÜNCHEN now comprises drawings and sculptures.

It would nevertheless seem appropriate to comment briefly on the model of *Broken Infinity* (Fig. 1), since the piece was so specifically conceived for the KUNSTRAUM MÜNCHEN that it will probably never be realized anywhere else.

The artist's intention was to install an endless strip in the shape of the mathematical symbol for infinity (Moebius strip), running through all the rooms in the gallery. Rather than being in one piece, the strip was to be manifestly 'constructed', using thick (7,8″ x 7,8″) wooden beams, the aim being to present a deliberately cumbersome structure whose visual awkwardness would contrast sharply with the elegance of the mathematical formula for infinity. The strip was to be mounted on simple wooden supports of varying heights, so that instead of standing on one level it would run up and down in space, thereby emphasizing its physical presence. Here and there, it would burst through the wall. The bold green paint on the wood was intended to form a stark contrast to the white of the walls. There was to be no vantage point from which it would be possible to recognize the whole as a Moebius strip; the spectator was to see only fragments of a mysterious structure which would require considerable effort in order to attain a perception of its formal unity.

This process of striving for a perception of form raises the philosophical and scientific question of infinity, of the shift from the visible to the invisible, from appearance to idea. Whilst individual human existence is finite, the cosmos still poses the question of infinity. Is our finity a fragment of infinity?

Plaise Pascal notes:
„When I consider the small span of my life absorbed in the eternity of all time, or the small part of space which I can touch or see engulfed by the infinite immensity of spaces that I know not and that know me not, I am frightened and astonished to see myself here instead of there . . . now instead of then. *Or like the memory of a guest who stayed for one day and passed on.* (The Wisdom of Solomon 5.15)[1]

The advances in scientific knowledge concerning the cosmos[2] have repeatedly exploded and revolutionized our general image of the world and forced us to revise the way in which we think about the universe.[3]

More and more, the fragmentary character of our knowledge of things is tending to produce a longing for harmony, for a unified vision which will embrace the entire cosmos, integrating all its parts into a perfect whole.

The majority of Michael Gitlin's sculptures consist of fragments, which are open to, and indeed require, augmentation by thought on the part of the spectator. The installation *Broken Infinity* on the other hand, would have shown a fragmented whole, a new departure in Gitlin's work.

Something of this sense of fragmentation is conveyed by Michael Gitlin's drawings. The lines, which constantly stop and start afresh, frequently attempt to assert themselves on a particular level. Other lines come in to oppose them, a conflict of levels ensues, and one receives the impression that the lines are trying to break away from the flat surface of the paper and move out into space. The lines at the front of the visual field shift into the background, from which other lines emerge and thrust themselves into the foreground. Their constant restless movement draws the spectator into the space which they define.

---

[1] Blaise Pascal, Pensées et Opuscules, Pensée No. 205, Leon Brunschwicg, ed., Paris 1961, p. 427, cit. by Rudy Rucker, Infinity and the Mind, Boston/Basel/Stuttgart 1982, p.2. (original text: Quand je considère la petite durée de ma vie, absorbée dans l'éternité précédente et suivante, le petit espace que je remplis et même que je vois, abîmé dans l'infinie immensité des espaces que j'ignore et qui m'ignorent, je m'effraie et m'étonne de me voir ici plutôt que là, car il n'y a point de raison pourquoi ici plutôt que là, pourquoi à présent plutôt que lors: qui m'y a mis? par l'ordre et la conduite de qui ce lieu et ce temps a-t-il été destiné à moi? *Memoria hospitis unius diei praetereuntis.* Sagesse, V, XV.)

[2] For an account of the latest advances in cosmological research, see Edward R. Harrison, Cosmology, the science of the universe, Cambridge University Press, USA 1981

[3] The ‚Big Bang' theory fails to account for what preceded the big bang (nothingness, a vacuum?)) or to answer the question whether the universe is expanding or, on the other hand, contracting and thereby tending to a state of nothingness.

HELMUT FRIEDEL

Die geborstene Linie

Michael Gitlins künstlerischer Zugriff geht prinzipiell von der Teilung aus. Seine Bilder aus den Jahren 1974 bis 1980 sind hinsichtlich ihrer Materialität zerborstene, gesprungene Holztafeln, deren Bruchkanten die massive Einwirkung von Gewalt deutlich erkennen lassen. Der Bildträger Holz verleiht den „tableaux" einen hohen Grad an Substanzialität, so daß sich die geteilten Bildelemente als Körper nicht nur in der Fläche ausdehnen, sondern auch im Raum zu emanzipieren vermögen. Zunächst heben sie sich reliefhaft von der Wand ab, verwandeln diese als Träger des Bildes in eine Folie, auf der sie agieren und die damit Teil der gesamten Bilderscheinung wird. Dabei spielt auch der Umstand, daß Michael Gitlin seine Bildtafeln vor dem Zerbrechen meist vollständig auf einer Seite monochrom bemalt, eine bedeutende Rolle. Indem er die Flächen mit einem schwarzen Latex-Überzug bedeckt, erhalten die so bemalten Tafeln eine graphische Wirkung, da sie sich kontrastreich von der weißen Wand abheben. Die Bruchkante wird dabei regelmäßig als Ordnungslinie begriffen, entlang der die Teile zueinander gekippt werden. So kann in einer Reihe von Bildern durch diesen Vorgang des Brechens und Umdrehens von Vorder- und Rückseite ein Nebeneinander entstehen, das auf die einfachste Weise eine räumliche Organisation von Tiefe angibt. Ausgehend von diesen Grundmöglichkeiten liegt die Expansion in den Raum sowohl hinsichtlich der Ausdehnung der Bildflächen auf den Wänden, als auch durch Zunahme des Volumens der Bildkörper nahe. In einer fast kontinuierlichen Entwicklung läßt sich daher beobachten, wie aus flachen Körpern auf der Wand Skulpturen werden, die sich von dieser abheben und in den Raum ausdehnen.

Zunächst bearbeitet Michael Gitlin solide Holzblöcke durch Schnitte, so daß Volumina gebildet werden. Die geschlossenen Blöcke werden dabei auf ihre Oberfläche, aber auch auf die in ihnen geborgenen Volumina, die sich im Inneren, gleichsam an den „Rückseiten" der Holzkörper manifestieren, untersucht. Dabei entstehen Gebilde kubischer Struktur, die aus massiven Klötzen und brettartigen Flächen bestehen. Stets bleibt aber die bemalte Oberfläche ein bedeutsames Element dieser Skulpturen. Durch Farbe wird offensichtlich, welches die ursprüngliche Oberfläche des festen Körpers war. Gitlin dehnt die „Bemalung" seiner Skulpturen in den Jahren von 1981 bis 1983 bis zu einer massiven, fingerdicken Schicht aus, wobei der Sinn der Ummantelung mittels Farbe besonders deutlich wird. Die Fassung seiner geschnittenen Körper wird so zur umhüllenden Schale, aus der sich das Holz wie ein Kern herausschält.

In den folgenden Skulpturen von 1984-85 scheint Michael Gitlin ausschließlich dem Weg gefolgt zu sein, bei dem er auf den Kern seiner Skulpturen als festes Material verzichtet und nur noch die Hülle zeigt. Aus dünnen Brettern baut er raumgreifende Hohlkörper, die allseitig bemalt sind. Diese neueren Skulpturen, die nun komplizierte

Figuren sind, die bisweilen splitterig aussehen, werden im engen Bezug zur Zeichnung entwickelt. Großformatige Blätter zeigen dabei kräftige, dunkle Linien, die sich auf dem weißen Papier gegen darunter liegende Malschichten klar abheben. Michael Gitlin scheint den weiß getünchten Ausstellungsraum als vergleichbare Folie für seine Skulpturen zu sehen wie das weiße Papier für seine Zeichenstriche.

In der Skulptur *Nostalgia* (Abb. 2), die Gitlin für das Kunstforum entworfen hat, greift er offensichtlich ein künstlerisches Prinzip wieder auf (Nostalgia?), das er in den Skulpturen zu Beginn der 80er Jahre entwickelt hatte. Von einem Sechser-Block massiver Holzbalken von jeweils mehr als 40 cm Seitenlänge, welche er hellblau bemalt, schneidet er Teile ab, die dann auf den Boden des Raumes gelegt werden. Die Expansion dieser Skulptur geht von einem soliden Körper, der mitten im Raum steht, aus und erstreckt sich über den gesamten Boden. Es bleibt zu warten, wie Michael Gitlin die Teilungen und die Aufsplitterung der einzelnen Elemente im Kunstforum zu einem übergeordneten Bild zu verbinden und ordnen versteht.

2   Nostalgia 1986, Modell

Nostalgia 1986

HELMUT FRIEDEL
The Broken Line

Michael Gitlin's artistic method is based on the principle of division. His pieces from the period 1974-1980 take the form of severed and broken wooden panels, whose rough edges bear the marks of brute force. The material itself, wood, lends these 'tableaux' a particular air of density and solidity, with the result that the severed individual sections of the pieces enjoy an additional spatial freedom beyond their surface extension. They stand out in relief against the wall, which forms a backdrop to the movement of the pieces and thus becomes a part of the overall pictorial effect. An important role is played by Gitlin's practice of painting the panels before severing them. The surface of one side is generally coated with black latex paint which contrasts sharply with the white wall and provides a graphic effect. The rough edge appears as an ordering line, along which the separate elements of the pieces are set at an angle to each other. In a series of these pictures, the manner of severing the wood is offset by the way in which the front and rear surfaces are alternately exposed, thus establishing, in the most simple fashion possible, a spatial organization of depth. Taking these basic formal possibilities as his point of departure, Gitlin's obvious next step was to expand his work spatially, both in terms of the surface area of the pieces and in respect to their three-dimensional presence. Hence an almost continuous development can be seen in which the originally flat surfaces take on the character of sculpture, turning out from the wall and extending into space.

At the start of this development, Gitlin uses heavy blocks of wood which are sawn into solid shapes. He is interested not only in the external surface of the shape, but also in the aspect of its volume, its underlying rear surface, as it were. These bulky wooden forms, with their board-like planes, have a cubist structure. The painted surface remains an important element in these sculptures; the paint is allotted the function of indicating the original outer surface of the solid body. Between 1981 and 1983, Gitlin does more and more of this kind of 'decoration', covering his sculptures with layers of paint up to an inch thick. The point of this practice becomes obvious: the outer coating of paint forms a protective shell, from which the wood beneath emerges like the kernel of a nut.

In his work from the years 1984 and 1985, Michael Gitlin would appear to have adopted and strictly adhered to an approach which involves dispensing with the solid core of his sculptures and only showing the external surface. Hollow forms are constructed from thin pieces of wood and painted all over; the pieces are large and spatially demanding. These more recent sculptures, which often have a fragmented look, are complex figures whose development is closely related to Gitlin's drawings. The bold dark lines of the large-format drawings stand out clearly on the white paper against the layers of paint on which they are superimposed. There is a parallel to be seen between the contrastive function of the white paper for Gitlin's drawing and the way in which he uses the white gallery walls as a background for his sculptures.

In his sculpture *Nostalgia* (Fig. 2), which was specifically conceived for the Kunst-forum, Gitlin returns (nostalgically?) to an artistic principle which he first formulated in his sculptures at the beginning of the 1980's. The basis of the work is a block of six wooden beams with a side measurement of over 40 cm, which have been painted light blue. Sections of the beams have then been sawn off and laid out on the floor. The sculpture thus extends outwards from a fixed body in the centre of the room and occupies the whole of the space. It remains to be seen how Michael Gitlin will use the space in the Kunstforum to order the discrete, fragmented elements of the sculpture and combine them into a central controlling image.

STEPHEN WESTFALL

Humanizing Sculpture

Michael Gitlin's work has altered considerably over the last several years but he has maintained a willingness to involve the viewer with the creation of each piece. In his sculpture and roughly physical plywood paintings (at least they appear to be more paintings than sculpture) from the mid to late 70s, the viewer could reconstruct a former whole from the fragments on view. In *Equilibrium* (fig. 3), for instance, he pares the sides most of the way down a massive square column of wood painted black. The cut away sections reveal a narrow core, also square, in its natural bright blond color. The four sliced sections are suspended on the surrounding walls at the same height as the column's remaining base. The black painted surfaces of the wood slats face the walls. Though the arrangement is almost ritualistically static, one has the sensation that the slats have somehow exploded off the original column.

The visceral quality of *Equilibrium* (fig. 3, p. 20), is felt not only through the evidence of work – the cut and tear into the wood (flesh) that the viewer participates in vicariously as he mentally reassembles the piece, there is also the matter of scale. The standing column, centered in the room, is taller than a man: a heroic figure. Its burst sides can be read as a metaphor for reach, the way dancers define their arena or a figure in the dark gropes for a switch. It is the crucifixion as an abstract choreography, a sculptural equivalent of Newman's Fourteen Stations. It was Newman who emphasized the importance of human scale (which had no bearing on actual dimensions) and he insisted that the requisite for such a scale was content. Content for Gitlin lies in the realm of the concrete. His pieces are not symbolic, and yet by triggering the perceptual mechanisms through which we reconstruct and project completion and by activating the muscle memory through which we recognize labor and the resistance of material, Gitlin manages to draw us out of ourselves. The building blocks of cognition are revealed to be steppingstones to an experiential, as opposed to a symbolic, metaphysic.

In the exhibition at hand, the maquette of *Broken Infinity* (fig. 1) offers a glimpse of a shift of emphasis in Gitlin's work. The green figure eight of painted wood bobbing and weaving out of the three adjoining rooms is in a presently completed state. Still, as before, the viewer must proceed to an image of the finished work in stages. Observers of the full scale work would be left in the role of the blind men describing an elephant from the part they each touched. The whole is extrapolated, again, from a series of fragments. Imagine the difficulty of moving around this piece. You'd have to duck and squeeze in order to even enter the middle room from the hallway. Everywhere the eye gazes, its effort to follow the movement of the work would be obstructed. When apprehension of the physically persuasive movement of the piece is interrupted, the jolt is physically felt.

Gitlin's later wall objects, more spatially aggressive wall/floor sculptures and, clearly, the recent oil stick drawings, have all moved to a more gestural format; approaching completion as it were, rather than decaying from it. The change in attitude could be noticed in 1981 pieces such as *Unpredictable,* with its series of oblique angled cuts complicating the viewer's perception of a reconciliation between the three blocks (not illustrated). The plaster-skinned *Sentinel* (fig. 4), *Exposed* (fig. 6) and *Doublecut* (fig. 9) abandon any pretense to rejoinment. The volume that would heal the exposed wood is absent. Gitlin has subsequently dropped any suggestion of subtraction, at least until *Nostalgia 1981-86,* the ironically titled major installation in the present exhibition.

The openness of the recent wall constructions and the near choreographic work on paper invite the observer to participate in immediate movement rather than reassembly. You can almost hear the slap of the wood slatting coming together in space in *Your Head or Mine* (fig. 19), while the gestural white areas in the drawings buoying his jagged and directional linear figures make space as palpable as a solid. The process of the piece arriving at its present state is as open to inspection as before. Yet the viewer is caught up in a forward-looking attitude as opposed to an elegiac one. Gitlin seems to know the difference, as the Orphic title of his large installation suggests.

Nostalgia (fig. 2) is clearly more reflective of Gitlin's earlier concerns. The rectangular columns bound together all have a piece cut out from them. Each fragment is laid out in the room and the spectator may recreate the original unviolated block. The light blue paint covering the outer surface of the columns (except, of course, where the cuts take place) playfully undercuts the massiveness of the bound structure. It is as if Gitlin has returned to his more classically minimal forms without presupposing their sobriety.

A work of art is essentially a perceptual machine. It sets off a chain of reactive events within the viewer's consciousness that may lead to contradictions as well as congruencies. But if it only does that then there is little difference between the artwork and a class science project. What makes Gitlin's work special is its coexisting attitudes of no-frills execution and stylishness. His art holds your attention by making reference to and awakening your body. Once attracted by the way the continuous, powerfully twisting limbs of *Broken Infinity* (fig. 1) mimic human musculature, it becomes easy to get caught up in the sweep of its configuration and axial alignments. You really want to do the work necessary to complete the piece in your mind's eye. And you can almost project a yearning to recover what's been lost among *Nostalgia's* (fig. 1) oddly heroic bound columns. I find myself sensing a poignant nakedness where they've been cut, and a slight embarrassment at having the inventory of their loss laid out on the floor.

Gitlin has found that rough-hewn wood warms and humanizes geometric form. This concern for humanization extends into the art situation itself. His work is a formal, abstract theater that integrates the viewer into the performance; elevates him, in fact, to the primary role in a human drama of perception unfolding into larger sympathies.

STEPHEN WESTFALL

Das menschliche Maß

Michael Gitlin's Arbeit hat sich während der letzten Jahre erheblich verändert, aber er hat seine Bereitschaft beibehalten, den Betrachter in den Schöpfungsprozeß jedes Stückes mit einzubeziehen. Bei seiner Skulptur und seiner einigermaßen körperlichen Sperrholz-Malerei (zumindest scheinen sie mehr Bilder als Skulpturen zu sein) von der Mitte bis zu den späten 70er Jahren konnte der Betrachter ein früheres Ganzes aus den ausgestellten Fragmenten rekonstruieren.

Bei *Equilibrium* (Abb. 3) zum Beispiel schält er die Seiten einer massiven viereckigen, schwarz gestrichenen Holz-Säule ab – fast bis ganz hinunter. Die abgeschnittenen Teile geben einen schmalen Kern frei, ebenfalls viereckig, in seiner natürlichen leuchtenden hellen Farbe. Die vier abgeschnittenen Teile sind an den Wänden drum herum aufgehängt und zwar in derselben Höhe wie die übriggebliebene Basis der Säule. Die schwarzen Seiten der Holzleisten sind gegen die Wände gewandt. Obwohl die Anordnung fast wie bei einem Ritual statisch ist, hat man gleichzeitig das Gefühl, daß die Leisten irgendwie von der ursprünglichen Säule abgesprengt worden sind.

Die innere Qualität von *Equilibrium* (Abb. 3, S. 20) fühlt man nicht nur durch die Offenkundigkeit des Arbeitsprozesses – hier das Schneiden und Reißen ins Holz (Fleisch) hinein, an dem der Betrachter nachempfindend teilnimmt, wenn er die Stücke gedanklich wieder zusammenfügt – es gibt daneben auch noch das Problem der Größenordnung. Die aufrecht stehende Säule genau in der Mitte des Raums ist höher als ein Mensch: eine heroische Figur. Seine abgespaltenen Seiten können als Metapher für Reichweite verstanden werden, so wie Tänzer ihren Bewegungsbereich festlegen oder wie eine Figur, die im dunkeln nach dem Schalter tappt. Es ist die Kreuzigung als eine abstrakte Choreographie, eine skulpturale Entsprechung zu Barnett Newman's „Fourteen Stations".

Es war Newman, der die Wichtigkeit des menschlichen Maßstabes betonte (der nichts mit tatsächlichen Ausdehnungen zu tun hatte); er bestand darauf, daß die Erfordernis eines solchen Maßstabes zum geistigen Inhalt gehöre.

Geistiger Inhalt liegt bei Gitlin im Bereich des Konkreten. Seine Stücke sind nicht symbolisch zu verstehen, und doch gelingt es Gitlin, uns aus uns selbst herauszuholen. Er löst Wahrnehmungsmechanismen aus, durch die wir die Stücke rekonstruieren und ihre Vervollständigung herstellen. Die Erinnerung an Muskeltätigkeit wird aktiviert, dadurch können wir die körperliche Anstrengung und den Widerstand des Materials nachvollziehen.

Die Bausteine der Wahrnehmung entpuppen sich als Stufensteine zu einer auf Erfahrung beruhenden (also nicht symbolischen) Metaphysik.

Für die Ausstellung hier gibt das Modell von *Broken Infinity* (Abb. 1) den Eindruck einer anderen Aussage in Gitlin's Arbeit wider.

Die grüne „Acht"-Figur aus bemaltem Holz, die sich auf und ab und im Zickzack aus den drei angrenzenden Räumen bewegt, ist in einem offensichtlich vollendeten Zustand, dennoch kann der Betrachter, wie früher schon, das Bild von der abgeschlossenen Arbeit nur Schritt vor Schritt erfassen. Beobachter der in voller Größe ausgeführten Arbeit würden sich in der Rolle von blinden Männern finden, welche einen Elefanten nach dem Teil, den sie gerade berühren, beschreiben sollten.

Das Ganze wird auch hier aus einer Folge von Fragmenten extrapoliert. Man stelle sich die Schwierigkeit vor, um diese Arbeit herumzugehen. Man müßte sich ducken und zwängen, um überhaupt den mittleren Raum vom Flur her zu betreten. Überall stockt das Auge; dessen Anstrengung, der Bewegung der Arbeit zu folgen, würde zum Erliegen kommen. Wird das Erfassen des körperlich überzeugenden Schwungs des Kunstwerkes schlagartig unterbrochen, empfindet man diesen Schlag körperlich.

Gitlin's spätere Wandobjekte als auch die – was den Raum angeht – aggressiveren Wand-/Boden-Skulpturen und deutlicher noch, die jüngsten Ölstift-Zeichnungen haben sich alle in Richtung auf eine mehr gestische Gestaltung zubewegt. Sie gehen eher hin zur Vollkommenheit als von dort her in den Zerfall zu führen.

Diese Einstellungsveränderung konnte man in den Arbeiten des Jahres 1981 bemerken, wie bei *Unpredictable* (o. Abb.). Hier erschwert eine Reihe schiefwinkeliger Einschnitte das Verstehen des Einklangs der drei Blöcke.

Die mit Gips überzogenen Arbeiten *Sentinel* (Abb. 4), *Exposed* (Abb. 6) und *Double-cut* (Abb. 9) verzichten auf jeden Anreiz, sie wieder zusammenzufügen. Die Masse, die das freigelegte Holz heilen würde, fehlt hier. Folgerichtig hat Gitlin jede Sugestion eines Wegschneidens fallengelassen, zumindest bis *Nostalgia 1986* (Abb. 2), der Installation im Kunstforum mit jenem ironischen Titel.

Die Offenheit der jüngsten Wandkonstruktionen und die fast choreographischen Arbeiten auf Papier laden den Betrachter ein zur sofortigen Bewegung statt zum Wiederzusammenfügen. Man kann fast den Schlag der Holzleisten bei *Your Head or Mine* (Abb. 19) hören, die im Raum zusammenstoßen, während in den Zeichnungen die gestischen weißen Flächen – die Gitlins zackige und gradlinige Figuren beleben – den Raum als festen Körper fühlbar machen.

Die Entwicklung des Kunstwerkes bis zum vorliegenden Zustand steht zur Prüfung so offen wie zuvor. Doch wird der Betrachter eher zu einer vorwärtsblickenden Haltung gebracht denn zu einer elegischen. Gitlin scheint den Unterschied zu kennen, worauf der orphische Titel schließen läßt.

Nostalgia spiegelt deutlich mehr Gitlin's frühere Anliegen wider. Von allen sechs rechteckigen, miteinander verbundenen Balken wurde je ein Stück abgeschnitten. Jedes Fragment wird im Raum ausgelegt, und der Betrachter kann den ursprünglich unverletzten Balken in Gedanken wiederherstellen. Die hellblaue Farbe, die die äußere Oberfläche der Säulen bedeckt (mit Ausnahme der Stellen natürlich, die herausgeschnitten wurden), unterhöhlt spielerisch das Massive des zusammengefügten Gebildes.

Gitlin scheint hier zu seinen mehr klassisch minimalen Formen zurückgekehrt zu sein, ohne dabei von deren Nüchternheit auszugehen.

Ein Kunstwerk ist im Wesentlichen ein Wahrnehmungsmechanismus. Es setzt im Bewußtsein des Betrachters eine Kette von weiterwirkenden Ereignissen frei, die sowohl zu Widersprüchen als auch zu Übereinstimmungen führen können. Aber wenn

3   Equilibrium 1980, J.C.C. Antwerpen

es nur dies täte, dann bestünde zwischen einem Kunstwerk und einem anspruchsvollen wissenschaftlichen Projekt nur ein kleiner Unterschied. Was Gitlin's Arbeit aber zu einer besonderen macht, sind die miteinander vereinten Standpunkte zur schmucklosen Ausführung und zur Eleganz. Seine Kunst fesselt die Aufmerksamkeit des Betrachters, indem sie auf seinen Körper anspielt und ihn ihm zu Bewußtsein bringt.

Ist man erst einmal berührt von der Art, wie die fortlaufenden, machtvoll gedrehten Glieder der *Broken Infinity* (Abb. 1) menschliche Muskeln verkörpern, so wird man leicht eingefangen vom Schwung ihrer Gestaltung und axialen Linienführung. Man wird richtig begierig, das Stück vor dem gedanklichen Auge zu vollenden. Und man ahnt den Drang, wiederzuentdecken, was von *Nostalgia's* (Abb. 2) seltsam heroisch verbundenen Säulen verloren gegangen ist. Ich selbst empfinde eine quälende Nacktheit dort, wo sie abgeschnitten worden sind, und eine leichte Verlegenheit darüber, den verlorenen Bestand auf dem Boden ausgebreitet zu finden.

Gitlin hat herausgefunden, daß roh behauenes Holz eine geometrische Form belebt und vermenschlicht. Dies Bemühen um Vermenschlichung erstreckt sich bis in die Kunstwelt selbst.

Gitlin's Werk ist ein formales, abstraktes Theater, das den Zuschauer in die Vorstellung einbezieht; es erhebt ihn, in der Tat, zu der Hauptrolle in einem menschlichen Drama der Wahrnehmung, das sich zu größerer Anteilnahme entfaltet.

4   Sentinel 1981/82

5   Revealed 1982

6   Exposed 1983

7   Green Counterpoint 1983

8   Push and Pull 1983

9   Doublecut 1983

10   Open Enclosure 1984

11 Encroached Arc 1984

12   Black Wall Piece 1984

13   Re-Cycled Fragment 1985

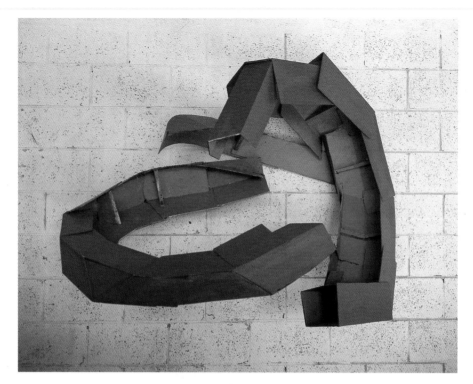

14   Space Link 1984

15   Yellow Bridge 1985

16   Accumulation Inside-Out 1985

17   Accumulated Headpiece 1985

18   Temporary Shelter

19   Your Head or Mine 1986

20   Fragile Sanctuary 1986

23   o. T. 1983

24   o. T. 1983

25   o. T. 1983

26   o.T. 1983

27   o. T. 1983

28   o.T. 1983

29   o. T. 1983

30   o. T. 1983

31   o.T. 1984/85

32   o.T. 1984/85

33   o.T. 1985

34   o. T. 1985

35   Installation, Mai 1985, Exit Art, New York (S. 52, 53)

Verzeichnis der Abbildungen / Index of Illustrations

15 Yellow Bridge, 1985
    Acrylic on Wood, 79″ x 126″ x 31½″,   220 x 320 x 80 cm

16 Accumulation Inside-Out, 1985
    Acrylic and Oilspray on Plywood, 50″ x 68″ x 46″,   127 x 172,7 x 116,8 cm

17 Accumulated Headpiece, 1985
    Acrylic and Oilspray on Plywood, 32″ x 22″ x 26″,   81,3 x 55,9 x 66 cm,
    Collection Catherine & Rainer A. Müller-Schmid

18 Temporary Shelter, 1985
    Acrylic and Oil on Wood, 23″ x 51″ x 63″,   58 x 130 x 160 cm

19 Your Head Or Mine, 1986
    Mixed Media on Wood, 50″ x 29″ x 29½″,   128 x 74 x 75 cm

20 Fragile Sanctuary, 1986
    Mixed Media on Wood, 48″ x 22″ x 39″,   122 x 56 x 100 cm

21 Installation, 1982
    Israel Museum, Jerusalem: Here and Now

22 Installation, Exit Art, New York, 1985

23 o.T., Untitled 1983
    Paintstick on Paper, 39″ x 50″,   99 x 127 cm

24 o.T., 1983, Paintstick on Paper, 38″ x 50″,   96,5 x 127 cm

25 o.T., 1983, Paintstick on Paper, 72″ x 63″,   183 x 160 cm

26 o.T., 1983, Paintstick on Paper, 72″ x 63″,   183 x 160 cm

27 o.T., 1983, Paintstick on Paper, 72″ x 63″,   183 x 160 cm

28 o.T., 1983, Paintstick on Paper, 72″ x 63″,   183 x 160 cm

29 o.T., 1983, Paintstick on Paper, 38″ x 50″,   96,5 x 127 cm

30 o.T., 1983, Paintstick on Paper, 39″ x 50″,   99 x 127 cm

31 o.T., 1983, Paintstick on Paper, 50″ x 38″,   127 x 96,5 cm

32 o.T., 1984/85, Paintstick on Paper, 50″ x 38″,   127 x 96,5 cm

33 o.T., 1985, Paintstick on Paper, 38″ x 50″,   96,5 x 127 cm

34 o.T., 1985, Paintstick on Paper, 38″ x 50″,   96,5 x 127 cm

35 Installation May 1985
    Exit Art, New York

Biographie / Biography

1943	Geboren/Born Capetown, South Africa
1963-1967	Bezalel Academy of Art, Jerusalem
1964-1967	Hebrew University of Jerusalem (B.A.)
1970-1972	Pratt Institute, New York (M.F.A.)
1984/85	National Endowment for the Arts Fellowship, USA
	Lebt/Lives in New York

Einzelausstellungen / Individual Exhibitions

1975   OK Harris Gallery, New York: 4' x 8' Series (Katalog)

1976   Schmela Gallery, Düsseldorf (Katalog)
         Stampa Gallery, Basel
         OK Harris Gallery, New York (Katalog)
         Bertha Urdang Gallery, New York

1977   Swart Gallery, Amsterdam
         Israel Museum, Jerusalem: Works: 1974-77 (Katalog)

1978   Schmela Gallery, Düsseldorf (Katalog)
         Primo Piano Gallery, Rome
         Stampa Gallery, Basel
         Swart Gallery, Amsterdam

1979   Schellmann and Klüser Gallery, München (Katalog)
         Gimel Gallery, Jerusalem

1980   Städtische Galerie, Erlangen (Katalog)
         Kunstverein, Ingolstadt: Works: 1974-1980
         Gimel Gallery, Jerusalem
         I.C.C., Antwerpen: Equilibrium (Katalog)

1981   Marianne Deson Gallery, Chicago
         Stampa Gallery, Basel
         Schmela Gallery, Düsseldorf

1984   Stampa Gallery, Basel

1985   Andre Emmerich Gallery, Zürich
         Exit Art, New York (Katalog)
         S-65 Gallery, Aalst, Belgium

1986   Kunstforum, Städtische Galerie im Lenbachhaus München
         KUNSTRAUM MÜNCHEN

Werke in öffentlichen Sammlungen / Permanent Collections

Brooklyn Museum, New York

Chase Manhattan Bank, New York

Fogg Art Museum, Harvard University, Boston

Guggenheim Museum, New York

Israel Museum, Jerusalem

Jewish Museum, New York

Kaiser Wilhelm Museum, Krefeld

Kunstverein Ingolstadt

Städtische Galerie im Lenbachhaus, München

Städtische Galerie, Erlangen

Stedelijk Museum, Amsterdam

Tel Aviv Museum, Tel Aviv

Wilhelm Hack Museum, Ludwigshafen

Wilhelm Lehmbruck Museum, Duisburg

Ausgewählte Gruppenausstellungen / Selected Group Exhibitions

1973   Brooklyn Museum: Pratt Prints

1974   Israel Museum: Beyond Drawing (Katalog)
Betty Parsons Gallery, New York: New Talent
Betty Parsons Gallery, New York: Collage

1977   Marianne Deson Gallery, Chicago
Documenta 6. Kassel (Katalog)

1978   Daniel Templon Gallery, Paris (Katalog)
Bündner Kunstmuseum, Chur, Switzerland: New York 78: Drawings of the Seventies
CAYC, Buenos Aires: Paper as a Medium of Expression (Katalog)

1979   Touchstone Gallery, New York: Paper Works
Galeria Belem, Lisbon: Lisbon International Drawing Show

1980   Bronx Museum of the Arts: Marking Black (Katalog)
San Francisco Museum of Modern Art: World Print III (Katalog)
Tel Hai, Israel: Tel Hai '80 (Katalog)
Schellmann and Klüser Gallery, Munich: Interior Sculpture (Gitlin, Nestler, Shapiro)

1981   Tel Aviv Museum: A Decade of Acquisitions
Mueller-Roth Gallery, Stuttgart: Lapidar (Katalog)

1982   Stampa Gallery, Basel: Drawings
Schmela Gallery, Düsseldorf: Anniversary Show
Israel Museum, Jerusalem: Here and Now (Katalog)

1983   Center Gallery, Bucknell University: Art For Your Collection

1984   Sculpture Center, New York: Ways of Wood (Katalog)
Alternative Museum, New York: Tit-For-Tat-Lin (Katalog)

1985   Tel Aviv Museum, Tel Aviv: Two Years: Accumulated Qualities (Katalog)
Kamikaze, New York: The Non-Objective World, 1985
Frankfurt Kunstverein: On Drawing 1960-1985, travels to the Vienna Museum of Modern Art and to the
Kassel Kunstverein (Katalog)

1986   Ivan Dougherty Gallery, City Art Institute, Sydney College of Advanced Education, Sydney, Australia:
Drawings From New York
John Davis Gallery, New York

Ausgewählte Bibliographie / Selected Biography

Art News. Vol. 77, No. 5. 1978, p. 63 (illus.)

Baker, Elizabeth C. "Report from Kassel: Documenta VI." Art in America. Vol. 65. No. 5. Sept.-Oct. 1977, p. 45.

Baker, Kenneth. „Michael Gitlin at OK Harris." Art in America. Vol. 65, No. 3, May-June 1977, p. 114.

Baruch, Adam. „Here They Come." Yedioth Aharonot, July 24, 1981, p. 25.

Baruch, Adam, "Gitlin File, 1981", Yedioth Aharonot, Sept. 11, 1981, p. 6.

Barzel, Amnon, Katalog Tel Hai Contemporary Art Meeting, Tel Hai, Israel

Bradley, Laurel. "Michael Gitlin." Arts Magazine, Vol. 53, No. 2. Oct. 1978.

Cardozo, Judith Lopez. "Marking Black." Bronx Museum, Art Forum, April 1980, p. 83.

Das Kunstwerk, Band 29, No. 3, May 1976, p. 56 (illus.).

Das Kunstwerk, Band 30, No. 3, June 1977, p. 13 (illus.).

Dienst, Rolf-Gunter, „Absolute Malerei." Das Kunstwerk, 4 XXXIV, 1981, p. 24 (illus.).

Excelsior, Seccion B, pag. 13, 9 de Abril de 1973 (illus.).

Fischer, Yona, Katalog The Israel Museum, Jerusalem, Works 1974-77, 1977.

Flash Art, No. 78/79, Nov., Dec. 1977, p. 10 (illus.).

Frank, Peter. "Michael Gitlin, Reviews." Art News, Vol. 72, No. 6, Summer 1973, p. 98.

Friedel, Helmut, Katalog Kunstraum München: Michael Gitlin, 1986.

Friedrichs, Yvonne. „Gitlin-Ausstellung." Rheinische Post, Sept. 22, 1981.

Friedrichs, Yvonne. „Michael Gitlin-Skulpturen." Das Kunstwerk.

Gentils, Annie, Katalog I.C.C. Antwerpen: Equilibrium, 1980.

Guisberg, Jorge. Katalog CAYC, Buenos Aires 1978: Paper as a Medium of Expression

Heinemann, Susan. "Michael Gitlin." Arts Magazine, Vol. 51, No. 7, Jan. 1977, p. 18 (illus.).

Kelly, James J. The Sculptural Idea, p. 82 (illus.).

Kesser, Caroline. „Michael Gitlin, Andre Emmerich Gallery." Tages-Anzeiger, Feb. 12, 1985.

Kunstforum International, Band 21, März 1977, p. 92 (illus.).

Kunstforum International, Band 26, Feb. 1978, p. 262 (illus.).

Levin, Michael, Trends in Israeli Art 1970-1980, Basel Art Fair 1980.

Lorber, Richard, Arts Magazine, Vol. 50, No. 9, May 1976, p. 23.

Madoff, Steven Henry, Katalog Exit Art, New York, 1985.

Manteul, Annemarie, Nationalzeitung, Feb. 1976: Basler Galerien, Stampa, M.G.

Nabakowski, Gislind, Lapidar, D+C Mueller Roth Galerie, Stuttgart.

Perrault, John. "A Smathering of New Talent." The Village Voice, June 20, 1974.

Pleynet, Marcelin, „Gitlin, Langlois, Nivollet, Pour une nouvelle abstraction." Art Press, No. 17, April 1978 (illus.).

Pleynet, Marcelin, Katalog Städtische Galerie Erlangen 1981: Works 1974-1980.

Raynor Vivien. „Where Black is the Primary Color." The New York Times, Feb. 10, 1980, p. 18.

Ratemeyer, Volker. „Fragen an das (Selbst-)Verständnis künstlerischer Medien." Kunst und Medien, Kassel, 1977, pp. 153-154.

Restany, Pierre. „Tel Hai 80." Natura Integrale, Oct.-Nov. 1980, p. 24 (illus.).

Ronnen, Meir. "The Age of Installation." The Jerusalem Post, Aug. 26, 1977, p. 19.

Ronnen, Meir. "Up in Arms." Art News, Vol. 77, No. 1, Jan. 1978, p. 129.

S.G. „Stampa: Michael Gitlin und Ulrike Rosenbach." Basler Zeitung, May 3, 1984.

Schneckenburger, Manfred. „Kurze Thesen zur Plastik der 70er Jahre." Documenta 6, Vol. 1, 1977, pp. 148, 178-179.

Stockebrand, Janni. „Michael Gitlin." Heute Kunst, No. 25, June-July 1979 (illus.).

Tacke, Christine, Katalog KUNSTRAUM MÜNCHEN 1986: Michael Gitlin.

Westfall, Stephen, Katalog KUNSTRAUM MÜNCHEN 1986: Michael Gitlin.

Turner, Norman. "Michael Gitlin." Arts Magazine, Vol. 51, No. 3, March 1977, pp. 34-35 (illus.).

Weskott, Hanne. „Michael Gitlin, New Works." Kunstforum International, Band 32, 2/1979, S. 223 (illus.).

Wexler, Max. „Michael Gitlin at Andre-Emmerich, Zürich." ArteFactum, Sept. 1985.

Zalmona, Ygal. „Michael Gitlin: Israel Museum." Maariv, sept. 2, 1977.

Zalmona, Ygal. „Location Direction '78" (Catalog of exhibition at the Ashdot Yaakov Museum, Sept. 6-Oct. 3, 1978).